VOLUME 3

Solos for Young Cellists

Compiled, Edited and Arranged by Cellist **Carey Cheney**

Art Design: Ernesto Ebanks
Cover Photo: Cello by Paul Schuback, Schuback Violin Shop,
Portland, Oregon, 1986; owned by Carey Cheney
Photo Credit: Elliott W. Cheney

© 2004 Summy-Birchard Music
division of Summy-Birchard Inc.
Exclusive print rights administered by Alfred Music
All Rights Reserved   Printed in USA
ISBN 1-58951-210-3

INTRODUCTION

Solos for Young Cellists is an eight-volume series of music compilations with companion CDs. This series is not designed as a method, but rather as a collection of wonderful music. This collection offers young cellists the opportunity to work in various positions, techniques, meters, keys and musical styles. These pieces provide exciting and diverse additions to the current repertoire. Many of the works in the collection are recognized as major repertoire pieces while others are newly published or original compositions. Compiled, edited and recorded by Carey Cheney, *Solos for Young Cellists* is a graded series of works ranging from elementary to advanced levels and represents a truly exciting variety of musical genres and techniques. The collection will become a valuable resource for teachers and students of all ages and levels. The piano track recorded on the second half of each CD gives the cellist the chance to practice performing with accompaniments up to tempo.

Contents

Romance

Transcribed by Alexandre Gretchaninoff

Claude Debussy
(1862-1918)

21030

2' 48"

Bourrée
Op. 24

W. H. Squire
(1871-1963)

Serenade Basque

1. Spanish Dance

Andrew Adorian

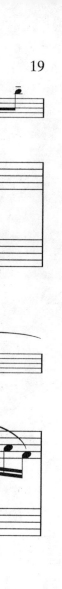

2' 10"

2. Poème

22

21030

3. Burlesque

Sicilienne
Op. 78
(Dedicated to William Henry Squire)

Gabriel Fauré
(1845-1924)

Sonata
in E minor, Op. 38, No. 1

Bernhard Romberg (1767-1841)
Transcribed by F. G. Jensen

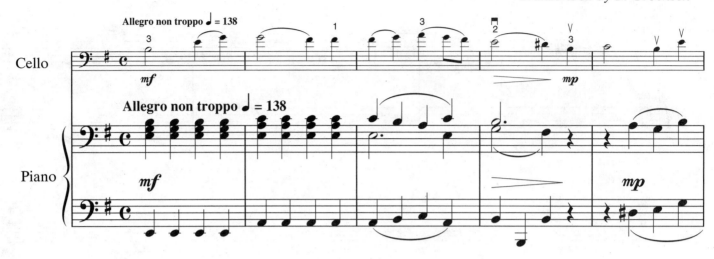

Sonata
in E minor, Op. 38, No. 1

CELLO QUARTET

Bernhard Romberg (1767-1841)
Transcribed by F. G. Jensen
Quartet arrangement by Rodney Farrar

*last 2 notes sound

21030

Fond Recollections
Op. 64, No. 1

David Popper
(1843-1913)

Harlequinade

W. H. Squire
(1871-1963)

21030

Humoresque
Op. 26

W. H. Squire
(1871-1963)

21030